salmonpoetry

*Publishing Irish & International
Poetry Since 1981*

ALSO BY RUTH O'CALLAGHAN

Wringing Blood (Salmon)
Mapping the light (Shoestring)
An Unfinished Sufficiency (Salmon)
Vortices (Shoestring)
Another Morning of Quiet Pleasures (Soaring Penguin)
The Silence Unheard (Shoestring)
Goater's Alley (Shoestring)
A Lope of Time (Shoestring)
Where Acid Has Etched (bluechrome)

Echoes From The Steppe (Soaring Penguin)

Without Skin: Interviews with 23 Internationally Renowned Women Poets (Soaring Penguin)

Ruth O'Callaghan
Unportioned
New and Selected Short Poems

This collection is published in 2019 by
Salmon Poetry
Cliffs of Moher, County Clare, Ireland
www.salmonpoetry.com e: info@salmonpoetry.com

Copyright © Ruth O'Callaghan, 2019

ISBN 978-1-912561-77-3

All rights reserved. No part of this publication may be reproduced or transmitted in any form or by any means, electronic or mechanical, including photography, recording, or any information storage or retrieval system, without permission in writing from the publisher. The book is sold subject to the condition that it shall not, by way of trade or otherwise, be lent, resold or otherwise circulated without the publisher's prior consent in any form of binding or cover other than that in which it is published and without a similar condition, including this condition, being imposed on the subsequent purchaser.

Cover & Title Page Image: *Photograph by Jessie Lendennie of a Mosaic by David Hill.*
Cover Design & Typesetting: *Siobhán Hutson*
Printed in Ireland by Sprint Print

for Christine
without whose love and encouragement
this book would never have happened

Contents

Prologue: Autopsy   11

from *Unfinished Sufficiency* (Salmon Poetry, 2015)

    A Calculation of Dark   13
    Whereupon   14
    Alterations   15
    Bury your own dead   16
    Narrative   17
    Vasilije: Christmas Eve   18
    Safari   19
    Stopping Place   20
    Of No Tomorrow   21
    Subsequent   22

from *A Lope of Time* (Shoestring, 2009; reprinted 2011)

    Villanelle – Pour Wine   25
    Visiting Time   26
    Letters in a Time of Nest Building   27
    Abendbrot   28
    Villanelle – Knew Her   29
    Apricots   30
    Incident in a Small Community   31
    What she said   32
    Inventory   33
    She hung the cord   34

from *Where Acid has Etched* (bluechrome, 2007)

    Ways of Grieving   37
    Entering Alzheimers   38
    Chronicle   39
    Killing Time   40
    Words of Water   41
    Bare light   42
    Cloths   43

from *The Silence Unheard* (Shoestring, 2013)

Filament	45
The Garden	46
Naissance	47
Scar	48
Transience	49
Night Garden	50
Brink	51
That Particular Coat	52
Child Game	53
Chelsea – '60s	54
Ghazal: For Certain	55
Slievemore: Deserted Village – Achill	56
Two Bays – Achill	57
Market – Achill	58
Cherry	59

from *Wringing Blood* (Salmon Poetry, 2018)

Antecedent	61
In Absentia	62

from *Vortices* (Shoestring, 2015)

Auspices	73
Blauschein	74
Source	75
Re-Creation	76
Death	77
Threshold	78
Dampen the Fire	79

Unportioned

	81
Prodigal	82
View	

Stray	83
Evanescent?	84
Prescience?	85
Always Dog	86
Firsts	87
Untitled 1	88
Untitled 2	89
Release	90
Locomotive Acts	91
Where?	92
After Her	93
Party	94
Returning	95
Encounter	97
Stable	98
Declension	99
Closure	100
Negation	101
Precipitation	102
Glass	103
Guest	104
Pliny: The Weight of Happiness	105
Beach Huts	106
Hospice	107
Beggared	108
Epilogue: To Whom It May Concern	111
About the author	113

Prologue

Autopsy

… and what of that no longer spoken?
Will it wait at the crease of each corner
in a slouch hat, bedraggled raincoat,
melt into walls, must thickening the air?

Or slip the sash on an unguarded window,
sidle into alleys less well-lit
where a grey fox noses through
the detritus of lives less lived?

Drawn by the clatter of aluminium bins,
will it stare out over wet gardens,
a rust of trees — what is that ache
that comes with rain? — wait for the long dawn

and the cat to carry in the thrush?

from *A Lope of Time* (Shoestring, 2009)

from
Unfinished Sufficiency
(Salmon Poetry, 2015)

A Calculation of Dark

In this ruined light – the dark leaking into the garden
as if the light were an interloper

whose presence, no longer desired,
is sequestered to other places – the urgency of shadow

conspires, determines cross-woven words that lie
in the gap between desire

and undisclosed restraints.
Such absence is mocked by the schack-schack of jay

concealed in the elderberry beyond the boundary wall
but a quiver of leaves betrays

as will a breath, caught,
or the silk-split of a leaf loosed from its stem.

Whereupon

What absence we sought in the loose
weave of light and shadow, eluded.

We could only wait out the long burn
of winter, each feeling the weight

of weather, folding each into himself
denying the sly making of small miracles.

Cocooned, we did not know whose grief
we held or who would listen to our plaint.

Mute, we only knew brute omission left
absence harder to bear than scourge

of stone: the fig-and-nettle broth of lies
that followed loss, hollowed grief to a reed.

Alterations

Light-boned, she had always been easy to swing over his shoulder
his hands deep in the taffeta of her skirt, her laughter high-pitched
she kicked then danced the air whilst he held her triumphant, aware.

        Aware, whilst he held her triumphant,
           she kicked then danced the air.
        She had always been easy, a swinger,
          had always looked over his shoulder.
        His knife deep in the taffeta of her skirt,
          her voice high-pitched, she was light.
                Boned

Bury your own dead

Do not ask me to bury your dead,
to pitch earth where worms sidle
amongst the ash and gob of him
whose drink-palsied hands clung
to the shovel, his sweat scalding
the mud and suck of a grief-hole
for one he never knew nor cared.

I'll not be there in mirrored shades
displaying loss in some false array
of plucked flowers, another's artifice
weaving wire through stems to form
a name so common the florist keeps
frames ready made but who agrees
grief that is so precious has no price.

You will not see me shadowing wall
or pew, black merged with black, hat
low, cuffing a tear, mourning her life.
I will not sit silent for false moments
recalling her laughter, compassion
or love. Do not ask me. I will remain
in our room holding her empty glove.

Narrative

Narrative? There is no narrative. Unless you mean
the mice-scratch of voices rising from the reeds'

silty bed or the latent lick of water rimming the bank
from a rower already beyond the curve of the river.

Yet ever, as the last harsh of the late returning crow,
deep-locked, shackles the evening, there remains,

unresolved but latched in, re-arrangements of light, air,
stealth, in a conspiracy of shadows, such a hunger

for the unremembered that even a midge or squall of dust
recalls maps of countries no longer named and those

who have no purchase trace, with naked eye, the plane's
arc prinked in the sky like stars in a child's colouring book.

Vasilije: Christmas Eve

He skirled towards me, a rasp and hawk of a man,
his mouth adrift in his face. He volleyed forth words

repeated over and over whilst inquisiting the shifting sky
the way you seek beyond the fluencies of light,

uncertainties inherent in the night's sequence:
the way shepherds scoured hills, on guard against wolves,

only to be ambushed by a hustle of angels,
by hallelujah upon hallelujah flinching still air

and that one star that even now hovers, uncertain,
above those precious wild words.

Safari

I have left linen bleaching in a white sun
by an inlet with its slack of winter water

where a heron breaks free from brittle light.
Skin tightened with cold desires the code

of touch. Unregarded, the curvature of trees
bears the mark of previous snows, grass

shrivelled, the earth bitten: winter-ravenous.
Winter-ravenous, I will arrive: my feet bare.

Stopping Place

Our eyes sly-slitted against a low sun
our wheels waist high
                    we devoured dust
scrub that gave way to cactii
trees and a ring of rocks
                        the boundaries of wolves.

We had learnt never to stop
even though the cab filled with his farts and the air
filled with the burnt warmth from the engine that lay
                                  between us
smothered with cloth

even though the rope-rigging
                    loosened
and the load began to shift and slide.

Where the valley narrowed
bone-white littered.
                Skulls. Some
ascertainable as cattle. Passing others
                          more familiar
we crossed ourselves, gave thanks for deliverance

but kept our eyes road-wise
    kept the cab close-closed against
                the cries of the slope-backed
old woman gathering slats, her home the four miles
we'd cover before her curses ended
        before the light's silvering
of olive trees, the fruit weathered.

In the shape-shift of garden
the well without a handle
                buried secrets
              deep
              black
              blank
              to the eye.

Of No Tomorrow

Was it summer we strolled in Grbavica, sat in the square
alight with fireflies, returned each night to strip

fish from bones, drink Slivovice from small glasses, the toss
of hands growing faster and faster before fumbling

back to our unmade bed, lips black from wine?
Waking to windows smoky in sunlight, hair straggling

a thigh and the sour smell of love?
Yet still we laughed while a laze of bees drowsed the days.

In lemon groves, the sharp of citrus in our throats or, tongues
salty with love on a spread of beach, we played

with doe-eyed boys. Harsh with hope we over-spent days –
September sun showed scavenging crows in ravaged fields.

Summer's faces retreated to the discreet of a dark that could not erase
the bruise of words, the past remained in grained photos,

albums on which to map memories. We turned leaves
but autumn failed us: sap-less trees in deserted streets.

Subsequent

It is the long sprawl of a late summer afternoon:
the pyrocanthus prickling the wall has not yet

the redness of berries nor white of flower
but bears a glint as a solitary finch pulses

the hours: the light lean in the tangle where thicket
smothers detail whilst absence smirrs

the first throat of darkness, dismantling the margins,
and grief's half-light leaves one beyond self.

Autumn will come soon over the mountains
bringing a thunder of flies with small stings.

from
A Lope of Time
(Shoestring, 2009; reprinted 2011)

Villanelle – Pour Wine

Pour me wine the colour of straw
let me unknow what I know,
leave words for words can say no more.

Call the priest, let him pray, restore
you to me, forbid you go:
pour me wine the colour of straw.

Lie close and from my mouth draw
your breath, take mine deep and slow.
Leave words for words can say no more

than years and years were never more
than love so, love, do not go:
pour me wine the colour of straw.

Lie closer still. Let us ignore
time, ask nothing, nothing owe,
leave words for words can say no more

than we have left unsaid. Yet your
breath fades, only the echo
(pour me wine the colour of straw)
leaves words and words will say "No more".

Visiting Time

My father's muscle slacked from the gap of the green gown
betraying the intimacy of this unknown man who had sat
wet-lipped, gleaming the glass of Guinness on his tongue,
railing against 'Black and Tans', potato famine, absentee landlords,
yet who, when the time arose, had shed civilian clothes, crossed
the Irish Sea to march against greater bully boys than Billy's Boys*.

This man who, when the dying cried for boats,
picked up his pipes and skirled that beach of no hope:
later he looked for lodgings behind closed doors:
                No dogs
                No Irish.

This man who couldn't fix the spoke of a child's wheel, mend,
with any certainty, a fuse or change the drip-drop of a washer
but who'd risked flak and fire to rescue a woman caught
            in her own high building
            behind her own closed door.

This man not fit for McAlpine's Fusiliers** – for how could you trust him
to lay foundations when the Sacred Heart stayed skewed on the wall? –
but who fastened a jacket close over frayed shirt, fashioned sleeves
into collar, borrowed a tie to satisfy Her Majesty's Post dress code.

This man, who even in memory, I cannot fit into a regular pattern,
whose roar was quieter than a dove's, his unspoken louder than words:
this known-unknown man lay with his last dignity taken away.

---

* Billy's Boys were the army of King William of Orange.

** McAlpine's Fusiliers were the army of Irish men who worked on the building sites after the Second World War.

Letters in a Time of Nest Building

Perturbed by scarves of rain travelling North
the Countess fled, entrained, she would declare,
to milder climes, Istanbul, Carthage, Zarzis,
holding forth, in lesser salons, on indiscretions
concerning weather. Inge writes from Garmisch-

Partenkirchen that despite the Führer's command
to join the two villages, no socialisation is allowed
between cows in public. Discovering after many years
at the *Institut der Aufklärung** that permanence
is but the absence of absence, Kenneth ended

their brief affair and has travelled to the virgin lands
of Japan with Mr. Saikaku Hirobumi to study Ikebana
before taking phenomenology: while we are here,
in this small garden, held ransom by a wren.

---

* Institute of Enlightenment

Abendbrot

Herr Gunther von Aschau, alone in bed,
attempts a perfect English accent, puckers
the unsuspecting air with vees and vowels,
misplaces each along with wallet, purse
last night's – sigh – Comfort Kitten, suppresses
thoughts of suicide by hanging, preferring
to visit London which promises nothing
but an abundance of suburbs, drizzle,
the clatter of Japanese and starlings.

Donning opaque overshoes – *to protect
the patent of my leather* – he defies
the vagaries of snow-bearing clouds,
pants towards the glittering glass and marble
of Hotel Hardenbrau where from a recess –
recognised by Herr Gunther von Aschau,
familiar with the closed intimacies of death,
zizz of flies behind curtains in darkened rooms –
a yellowed hand receives his dampened clothes.

Beneath the clock's face, black-nipple-pocked
for numbers, he speaks of the incontinence of leaves
to the snap-eyed waiter, studies his companion,
deems the evening to merit a mere Meursault,
salmon with a hint of lemon, its tartness
unmasked by the pleasantries of vegetables.
Sated, serviette to lips, he smiles, peruses
the dessert menu: tonight's youth seated opposite.

Villanelle – Knew Her

I thought I knew her yet I never saw her face,
hidden by hair or people in the gallery,
perhaps we'd met in a different time or space.

If carefully closed doors become displaced
is there any safeguard against catastrophe,
I thought. I knew her yet I never saw her face

but is that knowledge? Or loss? Or has time misplaced
joy, small sorrows, or was it through some tragedy,
perhaps, we'd met? In a different time or space

we were firm friends, lovers, refused others' embrace
and even then, though I never saw her clearly,
I thought I knew her. Yet I never saw her face;

although when dusk drifts from the river I retrace
each street we walked in this city where, both lonely
perhaps, we'd met in a different time or space.

Her age remains the same, now as then, as I chase
past portraits and people in this long gallery:
I thought I knew her yet I never saw her face,
perhaps we'd met, indifferent to time or space.

Apricots

        were scarce that year
but jalapeno chillies tumbled
from rush baskets, sprawled
on marble slabs in downtown
cocinas where 'roaches ran
or lay with wrinkled beans
in an earthenware pot
on the Yucatan peninsula:
Paco placed pieces on his bar,
patrons scooped whole handfuls –
tequila diminished the difference
between tears and rain.

A flush of early peppers waited
to welcome the striped bass
battered in sea sweat
that Ramos would bring
in the absence of orchids.

Incident in a Small Community

That night there was snow-light bearing hard cold
to crisp cotton sheets, the crump of men's boots,
voices rasping against the bitter air the same name
over and over in bass, baritone but not belly deep
as the moan of the woman anticipating loss,
while the father waited, wordless, to comfort her.

That night, just beyond the edge of their farmlands,
taking direction from a spine of trees, they climbed
Stoneseat, Rushdown, came to Havenmoor
and a mound roughly covered, untouched by foxes,
the same length as the girl-woman who'd teased
each of them, thinking she knew the measure of each....

But because the men did, having fought together
at a time when life was cheap and skirt cheaper,
to this night each man avoids the others' eyes,
each remains apart scything his own narrow strip:
each prays that that night a stranger had passed.

What she said

on her bicycle

Daddy, I can fly!
No, it didn't hurt.

at the doctors

A pinprick to make me better?
No, it didn't hurt.

on being told a story

Like mummy, daddy?
No, it didn't hurt.

Inventory

Behind the kitchen door, an apron, striped.
On the worktop an avocado, over-ripe.

By the board, blouses neatly stacked,
four still, discreetly, in cellophane packs.

In the wardrobe suits hang by dresses:
one rail's depleted, its weight lessened.

On the bedside table a photograph,
regimental tie, pin, Oxford college scarf.

In the bag, powder, light pink,
broken remains of extra strong mints.

Under the bed a satin mule, crimson madder,
two empty bottles, tights, discarded, laddered.

Over the banister a length of silk, shot
with blues and greens, doubled, knotted.

She hung the cord

on the same rail
her husband had hung

testing its strength
with her weight
as her husband had…

from
Where Acid has Etched
(bluechrome, 2007)

Ways of Grieving

Perhaps we should grieve
                        as elephants grieve

holding the bones
                    of our ancestors
close

in clear air
         where a drip of light
                    that falls between trees

catches the leaves' rustle
                    before rain

the muted croo-croo of doves
                        in shadows
where the river winds

         or watch in the snowlight
for stars

             paled
in a winter sky
            that casts beyond
what is known

           how ice cracks in the dying
fall of night

                  or how elephants tread
marvel at whiteness
                                          Light   Bone.

Entering Alzheimers

From the far shore where the herring gulls bred
he turned without understanding their cries
to search for something that he remembered.

Like the twining of fingers as she led
him to watch the rain skeining the skies
from the far shore where the herring gulls bred.

The dread in her eyes as their bodies, sated,
cooled in the night air. Now her face, misplaced, defies
his search. Something that he remembered?

Thoughts that would not untangle, that fled
with the flash of fish silver-slipping by
from the far shore where the herring gulls bred.

When he tried to snare words, in their stead
came sounds without form, or if formed, disguised
his search for something that he remembered.

Now, unclear, fearing that even when he is dead
memory, shape shifting, will not distinguish lies
from the far shore where the herring gulls bred
to search for something that he remembered

Chronicle

                    …On some days
a plash of oars
    breaks
the sleek of water

and a ripple will rim towards us
                eddying outwards
                  in ever fainter circles

as history once so delineated
pales into uncertainty

under layers of time
            of stories
                told   re-told
chinese whispers

                that hang in the air
re-defining dynasties   empires
              the cartographers' art

begun in playgrounds
        where children edge
           blues and reds
    making squares triangles
    in cheap colouring books

so occupied with such small tasks
           that the unseen oarsman
— had you forgotten him? —
            rounds the bend

while beyond
where willows sweep
           the water
and shadows under trees
    remain motionless

hanks of mist
        unravel
like sleeves of shopgirls
           reaching out
in the narrowing of the day.

Killing Time

When the letter came she took a small knife
to the faded forsythia that had once thrust
deep yellow against their windows.

For his chemotherapy he refused
her offer of a lift leaving her bent
over shrivelled daffs, binding them tightly.

Waiting, she cut dahlias, divided tubers,
scraped scales from lily bulbs
but at the thought of propagation

discarded them. The day of his operation
she made incisions in pliable stems,
stripped side shoots, tore at petals. To kill time

she hacked two flowering yew branches
which obscured the view of the river.

Words of Water

i.m. Dr. David Kelly

Which poet doesn't write in words of water
distilled from air in the thistle dark of night
where shadows of wings beat each thought

her mind forms, according them the same sleight
a conjurer constructs, contorts, discards?
Which lover doesn't use words to incite

love, each gesture maintaining the charade
strictly until the lover's passion's spent
and cold dismissal reveals the facade?

If poets and lovers are so intent
and words like weeds sway in their silted bed
trapping the unwary, then those so bent

that they play on fear can leave truth unsaid
and refuse to count the uncounted dead.

Bare light

"I hear those voices which will not be drowned"
    Written on the Benjamin Britten memorial on Aldeburgh beach.

Bare light and already an arm arcs
a half halo as a swimmer breaks
the waves, turning from the horizon, turning
shoreward towards guests unsnarled from sleep,

towards McCready, his skin taut as he curves
that same razor his father angled
against a cheek, gun-butt hollowed,
eyes narrowed down the sightline,
his bullet head close-cropped.

McCready razors his reflection:
his child-dark trek in the snoring hours
of backstreet lodgings (to slip on piss
two flights down) recedes into the marble
of this en-suite bathroom where he caresses

the crest on the Mercedes keyring, shrugs
into his silk jacket as the swimmer turns again
towards the horizon, turns from the memorial
whose words McCready has yet to read.

Cloths

One for the damp and one for the buff:
the beeswax crimps the nose of the child
watching as dulled wood emerges sheened,
the dirt dissolved and the firelight flickering

a mirror where a single column of elms vanish
into the horizon and a swing skews, its frayed rope
a thread from breaking. Here the hedge is broken
by a child crawling through, wood-mould,

green-mould clinging to knees and his clothes chafing
while he chalks each elm then every other, one in three, five
and his eyes narrow and a dust of snow turns into frozen fields
and the marks he made fade. Now there are no ashes

on ice to rough the path to the house where a smudge
of darkness presses against the window as an old man
discards his cloths, his breath blearing a mirror that shows
        a child, a child, a child dimininishing.

from
The Silence Unheard
(Shoestring, 2013)

Filament

A whisper. Not for the ear to comprehend but lower
perhaps ankle high...no, lower

an unknown operator moving through grasses
where home and light are finely attuned

metastable, eluding even the cat's whisker
that filches waves

filters air's turbulence, static, white noise.
Fine as a thorn

it catches the roar of the crowd beneath the balcony
the wash of water....

The Garden

A glint
severs the night
its edge sharp

enough to cut wind
also brings
a rustle of words

indistinguishable
from air sighing
through cypress

yet distinct
from the soft suck
of lips on skin.

Naissance

Only the sound beyond the ear's reach
beyond silence, soothes.

Washed by constant waters
remembered, later, in the touch of wind on skin

in that first exhalation, first greeting
first knowledge of lying

outside the silence
the voice is heard, an instrument

whose sharps and flats desire interpretation
the rough bark startling

— as it still does —
indicates love or its faithful companion betrayal:

a kiss sword-sharp given in a midnight garden
a sop of vinegar-wine

— not a malicious act —
a rock rolled back, an empty cloth where hope also lies.

Scar

A scar, visible
catches light

smoothes skin
or its absence

for what is hurt
burnt

is not renewable
but replaced
as light, caught.

Transience

Snow falls stealthily, frugal, does not settle
on leaves wet-bright

the way sun after rain dazzles the eyes.
It will always be this:

a scripture of sun, voices drowsing beyond
the window

and, later, rain snaggled
in her hair, the church quiet in candlelight

years where blessings held fast
before grief held close and the snow treacherous

the afternoon white and none to call a name
none to hear a name called

or witness the constancy
of these snowdrops in winter's early darkening.

Night Garden

A rainless night despite the forecast
with the dusk coming quickly, heaving against

the open window to fill the room with a migration
of vowels, syllables, whispers

hidden in the litany of leaves of this November dark
whose soft force disengages each browned stalk

from the tree's branch, the seed of which you buried,
at last, in an unyielding ground.

Now the blackness of trees fills the garden
and the chill of earth is as then.

Brink

Darkness did not play a part though
you'd have thought it would. Outside
a rose swayed in a slight breeze,
a bud unfurled a little in the warmth.
Inside, your eyes open, the edge
of the bed sharp beneath buttocks
and the knowledge upon you, and yes,
there was cold, cold that seeps
from forehead to nape to feet.

        Perhaps
forgiveness should be sought or found
in the polish of old furniture, the scratch
restored to smoothness, the re-lining
of wooden shelves. Perhaps in such
lies the eternal. Yet, as still light banded
the garden, it inhabited the room, crept
between sheets and the day's *De Profundis*,
the sun slant through French windows,
  the cat slinking the glass.

That Particular Coat

                          – leather/slashed –
one would expect to be worn wide

open with a raked beret but you were
close buttoned yet so thin you moved

inside its movable room, close connected
hotel, lobby, bar, a stranger's suite, bus

station, setting hope down in smaller
corners, splaying on narrow beds, grey

nylon sheets. A button went first, lost
in the basement of a bed and breakfast

whose landlady disinfected daily the one
toilet on the second floor landing. The buckle

broke in the amusement arcade, playing with
pennies until the hostel opened. A tear

unnoticed left the faded lining showing, a thread
of grime hidden in its seams led to the rip

which crazed a pattern on the back down to the
sagging hem, the belt dragging the river bed.

Child Game

A woman, young, still by the open window.
It is Saturday. Rainless. Dark has closed.
Coming quietly. Blue then black. Cold blows
lifting skin on her bare arms. She does not
reach for the lamp's protective light but filters
the usual night sounds: dulled roar of traffic;
a siren edging through; the rattle of shutters;
goodnights in other tongues; a voice, hoarse
with drink and cheap cigarettes, wheedling
children to bed, urgent to leave. The judder
of door. Silence. Then a wail, barely formed.
Fingers knit over her stomach. Cat's Cradle.
She's never able to complete the final twist.

Chelsea – '60s.

Only a forgotten grief remains: basement, Gauloises, black girls who clicked their fingers, slowly, marking their own music with soft cries and crimson nails, leaving no future desire....
                      Lent brought other, cloistered, places, repentance, whispers, but the slick flick of beads did not still an ache for sunlight bright on a pavement, tables in a street where a woman loiters, seeking solace from the bitter dark coffee she swirls incessantly, the bowl white as the lilies she laid on a child's grave.

Ghazal: For Certain

A string of dark drags across the river,
longing for absence she knows she'll leave her
                                      for certain.

In a small town a man wakes, smiles while his wife dreams,
smoothes lines from her face yet knows he'll deceive her
                                      for certain.

For better or worse tends to the latter – but what matter?
It's lethal but legal to propose a prenuptial – words are never
                                      for certain.

A waiver, disclaimer, howsoever it's written
warns of intent so bind him before or after he'll slither:
                                      for certain.

Some promise passion then leave with sweet words
when all passion's spent a sliver of silver delivers
                                      for certain

Will the heart that sighs, cries, is faithful, true,
be betrayed despite its best endeavour?
                                      For certain.

Then why carve my initials in this rock
if only death proves the lover which time cannot sever,
                                      for certain?

Slievemore: Deserted Village – Achill

In summer's long light they laid rooves to guard their nights
against scouring winds, built walls thick against snow and sun:
fed hens who cackled eggs splotted with warm shite, rubbed
on skirt or *báinín* apron, to be bobbled in water, rag-packed
and pushed deep in pockets of men who followed field walls
running downhill on the south slope of Slievemore, believed to be
His face made manifest. May His blessings be abundant this day.

Horses stood, faces turned to the stone, or laid their necks,
each across each, for here warmth is all, before submitting
to harness and the clopper over stones to Tuar, Tuar Riabach
or Faichee, the potatoes showing small and hard in shallow soil,
the same soil that yielded oats and barley for the making of bread
and rye whose plaited ropes held fast the thatch on rooves
as God's hand tore across the land and thunder was His voice.

Cattle moved on the mountain, tongues twining the grass
as men tended new plantings, the land striped and each stripe
mingled among others, leaving neighbour beside neighbour
ready with tool or word or the carrying of the coffin after a full life
and the cross whittled with love. Blessed are those who knew
not the sucking of stones to hold the hunger within: those deeds
of God made manifest. May His mercy be abundant this day.

Two Bays – Achill

Keem Bay

How easy to hear the harpist plucking gently
beneath the drum of wave, each note restrained
as surf turns from shore, the fingers fine-boned
and hair, for there must be hair, trailing back
black and loose. Perhaps, listening close, she,
for it must be she, keens, the sea grazed
with her hymn which the wind steals, sweeps
over kelp and sedge to appease Slievemore
where hunger lies yet in the broken stones,
in the bruise of light when the people fled,
leaving the tide to come and go like grief.

Girl: Keel Bay

It was the way to walk the beach, the sand hard
beneath spread toes, pedal pushers clung tight
as rain drove in, the head bare and face uplifted,
a small dog running beside. She'd pick a stone,
the size right in her hand, her fingers clasping
the smooth roundness of it, bend to wash clear
its silt at the sea's edge, tilt it toward the light
for a glow of amber, green or the thread of red
making this stone, this particular stone, her gift
to balance in her palm, to feel the exact weight,
to arc through the air heavenwards, homeward,
her eyes, the colour of shale, following, red hair
falling, a drape of seaweed against bare shoulder.

Market – Achill

Each purchase entered by hand in a thick, black book
that recorded individual endeavours and set beside
the corresponding number an amount paid, the flat stroke
of a one or a fat eight, each carefully inscribed in ink
by Miss Condon who'd taught five to ten year olds the art
of hemming handkerchiefs. Her nib never known to cross,
she'd purse lips that had dealt the withering phrase
about a cobbled corner or a tacking stitch stretched
too far, as each fine stroke denoted how her once-charges
were spending their days. On the box a nine tallied with eggs,
a splat of feather attached, brought to market by Mary Mack
whose neck was always tide marked, her name given
in the surety she'd never be able to spell a longer and so
repeated at confirmation and assembled children chanted Mary,
Mary-Mary beneath the baritone of the priest leading the rosary.

Twelve showed the plum jam of little Nora whose copy
was never blotted unlike the thirteen of Siobahn O'Flaherty
whose hair flew from her pigtails the boys loved to pull,
whose fists flailed frequently and who'd, Miss Condon noted,
added whiskey to her marmalade. No surprise with her upbringing.
Sea kale to cure infirmities, fossils and starfish splayed
by the number three that was beach-combing Danny Flynn
whose attendance had been so poor he'd never learned
to turn a corner but who'd waited at the gate every day,
a shell in his hand for shy Serena, she whose tiny jumpers
were for sale or giving, she cared not which, since the knitting
of them proved to be in vain. No number was allotted to her.

Cherry

So unexpected.
That redness!
In a side road. In a suburb.
And there just to be taken.
                                          Plucked.
I couldn't help but   reach out.
Oh, it came readily enough. But not soft.
It's hard shininess an angry demand
not to be found wanting. To be tested
                                            al
                                           dente.

I rolled it over my tongue
savouring
the feral-ness of it
in this place of lace curtains.
Rolled my tongue around it
testing gently with teeth
until it released juices
that steeped me with sweetness.
Wild, you said. *Wild*.

from
Wringing Blood
(Salmon Poetry, 2018)

Antecedent

Those kisses you placed upon my cheek
first left then, adroitly, right, were formal
as an English handshake upon greeting
upon leaving behind.

                      And you, uncertain
loath to go, unable to say what lies between
swoop, catch the corner of my mouth, naked
                                eyes open.

                      Behind lies
the late night ferry pulsing in safe harbour
Barreiro's distant lights waiting to welcome.
I wanted wilder waters and you.

In Absentia

Vital this opening. You mail from Lisbon and my silver
Apple conveys the news. Outside, the pointed cypress
pierces a skin of sky, of cloud while, waiting, mist falls
the way the unexpected contracts all to the immediate.

Distance deters contact. Stricken, I know we cannot be
fellow travellers but knowledge is never acquiescence.
In that dark place silence ruled: we never owned a song
that may chance from some balcony, the woman unseen

behind blue bougainvillea. We had only currency spent
in days, months, years apart – a part is less than whole
so I will gather you to me, give you the narrative I travel.
We will elude all others. In our winter, this is our spring.

2.

Here it is spring. We live in different seasons. Indifferent
seasons have passed but now your mail is a promised
slice of light read beneath this close-closed cypress.
We too will be close but not closed nor sway, as it does

in the slightest wind. Ineluctable, we will refuse confined
spaces. Our time has passed: we have only the remnant.
Let there be no regret but let us not be makers of myths
lest we become victims, once again, to old proscriptions

barred, this time, by our own creation. Unplanned talk
unmasks. We will deny all casuistry with uncorseted
words until we both quiver — taut as bow-touched strings
my tongue plucking each place where you rush for refuge.

5.

Without, burnt earth reflects brown-bright
as the evening's dusk lends its last light
to shimmer unripe olives in this Tuscan air quick

with birds. Our bus rolls through the cleavage
of hills, not Housman's blue remembered ones
(such blue remembered hills!) but lightened by

a flick of hares kick-boxing in mad-March spring.
Headlights shine into our darkness. We are coming
soon to riverless Siena where the water is constant.

In another place the cracked earth yields its roots.
In another place, taller, erect, you stood over me
your shadow falling exactly on mine, travelling beyond.

8.

You tell me how the bees your father kept, swarm
form a new colony when unable to sustain desire

for a sovereign remote since winter's huddle: the hive
unable to sustain the warm spring increase, conceive

a new queen leaving the old to seek, with loyal subjects,
a different residence without dwelling on her past.

I tell you how my Grandmother died playing football,
not premier league, you understand, but from her chair,

never failing to retrieve, return. She lacked any desire
to die as other old declare they're ready, so we struggled

to keep the balloon floating between us: light as our words
relating insignificant incidents within these Sienese walls.

And then we talk of love, the impermanence of desire:
ignore our accidental rub of shoulder against shoulder.

16.

Unmoored, I resort to distant days when distraught cries
blocked our path. A fledgling, beak wide open reveals bare
yellow of throat – knowing despair yet too naive to know
endgames come in unexpected places – its *dweep dweep*
on my urban ear strapped my feet securely as a lion's roar.

Country born, you simply said, *Poison pellets* and I, appalled,
sought a solution finding none in your retreating back: heard
Kindness would be to kill. No inflection. Acceptance essential.

The rock, exact in my palm, freed the bird.
                                                There was absence:
the blood and the water not apparent: only the complexity
of silence.
            Without turning, your hand, fine-veined, gripped mine.

13.

I gave you a book of birds but they were from a different continent.
I gave you a blue jumper too heavy for summer and not winter wool.
I gave you a curved boning knife, keenly honed. It sliced your hand.
I gave you a disc, *Amália, fadista, Rainho do Fado,* you had no player.
I gave you a flower found in a field of corn, you looked away.
You gave me a map where truth lay lying:
                                I send my poem to where truth lies dying.

11.

Have I been harsh? I said there would be no refuge
no respite from reality. We are hostage to our knowledge.

Even the sun adopts the warder's stance, secures us
to shade, our shadows no longer visible. Yet we are craven

willing to cross and re-cross the baked paving to admire
a Fra Angelico, Michelangelo in some small chapel yet refrain

from contemplating living pictures vivid behind eyelids
thinned by sun, by age. We are no longer young. We cannot be

touched by the dead. Let us sew them a new shroud to bury
old suspicions: their mouths' incontinence dribbling lies: for closure.

They cannot hold you, hold us, in thrall if you believe words
staked to this page bear true witness. Do not ask me to draw with water

that no mark of love will be left. We have paid our dues.
We are shriven. I will take the tire from your eyes, give you laughter.

14.

Rooted in life we never spoke of death
harnessed each day to the task in hand
marked our narrow life with simple words
selected from a mandatory tract: to elude
authority we transformed their meaning
into cryptic messages.
                      There was nothing
cryptic, nothing erotic, sent to my silver *Apple*
just plain fact to be read, re-read, re-read....

I printed it, twisted the paper to dislodge
words not wanted. No desire left, I slept
gripping it the way a child falls asleep
holding an empty glove which love
once filled, knowing absent fingers
                                  are his fault.

17.

Night's stain invades the light, windows deflect the dark
the way widows deflect grief until finally absence breaks.

Absence hollows my mind. Boned of speech, I wait out
a monochrome of days, a waste of days distinguished only

by the clack of tongues tourists spit. Saturdays it's Japanese,
rummaging amongst racks of Armani, Prada, Versace, D&G.

Monday/Tuesday older Italians arrive to jostle with Chinese
leaving mid-week for British who refuse all guidance, spend

unknown afternoons stricken with heat, wanting small
currencies of purchase, bargains to brag back home

with tales of drains, the sloe-eyed waiter. Interlopers,
they gather into bars, onto terraces, sip spritzers, grimace

over rough chianti as shadows lock the Piazza del Campo:
the year is too early for the *Palio*, too early for death.

19.

This is riverless Siena.
I will not pay the ferryman with tears.

I will not let grief fill this void.
I will not speak in words of watered silk.

I will write how you refused
to sip from my water bottle despite your thirst.

I will not write of regret
such empty words clatter as a spoon in an empty bowl.

I am empty.
I will don my collarless shirt, wring the neck

of the last bottle, leave for Riga
Antananarivo, Astana, Bujumbura, Mbabana…

I will not find you pleached with stars
but, perhaps, tilting against the light, I may see you

where the sun catches on rock
where a drape of rain obscures the hills.

from
Vortices
(Shoestring, 2015)

Auspices

They will learn: all knowledge will be theirs.
The shore will desert the sea, seek distance,
fish will offer themselves to indifferent gulls
that refuse the gift, preferring self mutilation,
cattle will skip on the road to the abattoir.
Man will remove the architrave of the cross,
take up his dread life from his needy friend
to dance on Golgotha: his steps will entice
the mouldered dead to rise as worms do
to the pattering of birds or a slur of rain.
Laughter will be their sorrow, sorrow their joy.
Wisdom will come from the mouths of fools,
the traveller seek refuge in unsafe places.

Blauschein*

I am blue. I bear no allegiance
to him who carries me from fear.
I am his life. Without me deportation
from starvation guarantees death.
This is the lesser of his two evils.
Lose me and life is grasping water.

I am passive. On request I show
my face, his face, to a hard face
that demands identification, laugh
as hard face throws me in the dirt,
the scrabbling hand stamped upon.

I am, you see, without morals.
When I was stolen, as he prayed,
I left the synagogue, its catalogue
of wails soon silenced. I am owned
by another now. I parade his face..
I am blue. I am passive. I am you.

* People, usually Jews, who were defined as 'Volksschädling' (vermin/harming the public) but who were deemed necessary to the war effort, were given a blue card that helped avoid deportation from the ghetto to Auschwitz/Birkenau.

Source

In the beginning was the word
and the word was with the women
who lean together like trees guarding precious water.
In the word was the beginning
and in the beginning was the water of being
and the word and the water were given to the women.
And the word was with hope
and the hope was in the women
and the women guarded what was precious in this place.
And being given hope, watered
with the word wherein the beginning lies
for how else could it come into being, where else
would genesis rest if not in the word?
Yet both the word and the women know
how hope lies as they lean together guarding this place.

Re-Creation

How these trees lean together like old women at the well
the water long drawn, the bucket slopping
the years straitened by black.

Each evening at sunset they gather here to dismantle
myths not of their own making, to rehearse
memories to perfection.

In this place love lies. Words empty in a clatter of leaves
fronds still wet with the sin of those who fumbled
under them seeking sanctuary from hope.

Forgiveness is given to those who sinned in spring
but not for those who tended summer's
olives other than their own.

Shriven, yet shoots still appear in unexpected places
despite boundaries of light, of water, sky
the frugality of air…

Death

places a lace handkerchief
over her nose, lifts her gown
clear of urine and other matter,
slowly rises through the stairwell.
She knows the ache for escape

lies on the tagged walls – the young
yet to realise the release she offers.
Her ringed fingers caress a scab
of steel: the handrail flakes.
On the fourteenth floor she slips

casually past the slick young man
whose smile reflects his work is done.
Death bends gently, notes
her silver bangles will not wake
the old woman. Death appreciates

the young man's art: commitment
to detail leaves the carpet unmarked.
Her dimpled wrist brushes a speck
of saliva as she adjusts the teeth
loose in the mouth. She closes her eyes.

Death does not dawdle.
She follows him across the arc of this city
to visit the righteous or the fashionista:
he does not differentiate.
His time is precious.

Threshold

She felt she was on the threshold
but feared the step over
did not know how to step over
was stopped each time
by the fear of the step.

      He saw her dilemma but could not help
      he knew he should but he would not help
      he waited for her decision, her indecision
      decided him to wait and see, leave her be.

It isn't the fear she wishes to shed
knowing no fear to be fatal
but the step, the step
leads to the fear
leaving her.

      He believes in her, she will hold her course
      she has held her course over all these years
      she has been steady, steadfast in uncertainty
      if now she steps in another direction he is ready.

Without the fear, without the step
she is naked.

      This he knows.

Dampen the Fire

Come, little one, in from the rain.
Rivers flood but we need blood's stain
                         to dampen the fire.

They curse the children, let them thirst,
deny them water, use their pain
                         to dampen the fire.

Pain is truth, truth is rare.
Martyrs burn. Forbid the profane
                         to dampen the fire.

They burn the books! Books are truth's bones!
Burn books or bones they try in vain
                         to dampen the fire.

Without words we are lost.
Where are the poets? All detained
                         to dampen the fire.

Then bring the priests, let them speak.
Will you listen to words ordained
                         to dampen the fire?

So come, little one, take my hand,
what falls from the sky is not rain
                         to dampen the fire.

But who can I trust? Where is truth?
I live in truth. Truth knows it's insane
                         to dampen the fire.

Unportioned

Prodigal

if i wrote to you as often
as i spoke to the thought of you
it would show these lost years
have not been all cold, knowing
that at the very catch of winter
you have been there
holding a scarf or gloves,
keeping open the door.

i.m. Mary Chiappe née Loddo
22nd May 1939 – 8th December 2017

View

Engineers have reclaimed the land beyond your window:
if I had not felt the slow pulse of your life drain

if I had not watched the line fail, flatten, not even the slightest
spike let alone one sharp enough to pierce

the earth you have chosen no longer, in your wisdom, to trespass
or seen the cannula that needles you morphine

until your light, burning all night in the side room, finally fades
would your ghost, this snowfall

white as noise, that travels with me no matter which way I turn
no matter how I try to step past, search

for me on the wrong side of our history?

Engineers have reclaimed the land beyond your window.
They began before you needed the view.

Stray

I should have thought.
I should have said *Perra*.
Perra, Mary. *Aquí hay
una perra perdida.*
Then you would have stayed.

A fishhook in tongue,
eye pierced with thorn. See.
Her ribs, her dugs shrunken,
the ear hung half loose. *Perdida.*

I should have thought.
I should have said *Muchacha*.
Muchacha, Mary. *Aquí hay
una muchacha perdida*
Then would you have stayed?

Evanescent?

Our long distance relationship could never last.
Oh, we set out our promises, made dates aided
by i-cloud, flew to places one or other happened
to be – Mayfair, Main Street, our *own quiet space
at Gatwick before security. If L-I-F-E* very rudely
intruded in form of family, work, kids – the normal
pick up, drop off – pets, vets., unexpected guests
when household gods decree it's freezer failure/
boiler breakdown/car crash time or, probably, all
three, insurance lapsed, we never winced, never
even flinched as the web collapsed, simply sent
cards, wrote letters or swapped cautionary tales
on that same 'phone you used to break the news:
enough is enough you determined: refused food,
any liquid, all meds. except morphine: faced away.
It has only been 58 years. I counted on another 20.

Prescience?

In one way it wasn't long.
                    The phone call on Wednesday
informing of this Friday expectancy. You delivered exact.

Looked at in another light
                    that of a summer, hectic
with the move from Manilva, the new flat two flights up

from the one where you began
                    the process was slow, painful
though you refused to complain but hefted yet another box.

Did you think, like that other Mary,*
                    In the end is my beginning?
Did you know? Was it why you chose to settle the family

in the community familiar
                    since childhood, adolescent escapades
recounted to callow grandsons, daughters ooh-ing over a bride

as beautiful as you who
                    now lies in this hospital bed: will absolute?
I grasp your hand. I cannot grasp your wish for this last act.

---

* Mary Queen of Scots embroidered *En ma Fin gît mon* Commencement before her execution.

Always Dog*

You gave me

*An always dog who never were
nor will but might have been.
He chewed and gnawed coroningly
through mental forest bones of prose.
Perhaps he were my always dog.*

I gave you…?

---

* Mary scribbled this on a serviette – I assume it is her own verse.
If it has another provenance, many apologies.

Firsts

And who will now tell our back story?
Without you there will be no correction
of memories drawn in different minds –
that first time you slipped on ice, rising
gracefully as a novice from genuflection.
The endless streets we walked, ciggies
we shared in a Putney pub where you,
seven years older, bought our first cider,
forgot the crisps, and then on Monday
we went back to being pupil and 'Miss'.

The letter you wrote, the way you spoke
of love, *not candy floss, not red roses.*
Yours was pure tungsten, no ifs no buts –
well, yeah, there were *butts*. Your proposal,
a trip to Gib., was bad luck for Bill so soon
after the honeymoon, I suppose, but, hell,
it happened, the three of us survived though
now only two of us are alive to tell the tale,
to try to reconcile our loss: if it be your will,
so be it: Our Cross. That letter. I have it still.

Untitled 1

That day nothing happened. A threat of gulls bluster
as the lift of wind drags wings towards the Rock:
an icon on God's computer.

Beyond the window a cluster of small boats
stooked by the harbour wall wanted release:
wheat waiting for the reaper.

Sirens grieve through streets alive with workers,
beggars, shoppers, litter, the usual pollution:
city life, city death.

Inside a squall of nurses flood the room landscaped
with machines, with life, with death: your choice.
Nothing happened. Everything did.

Untitled 2

This is our final act. No loving words. No words.
No reclamation, for who can reclaim past nuances:
a look, the casual smoothing of collar en passant
or quirk of lip as the unstated word, quiescent, lies
between us.
                Silence is our antiphony. Crab-like,
fingers scrabble your inert wrist in the covert hope
touch will subvert your charting of this passing day.
Beyond your balconied window the wind riffles
leaves, reveals
                    woodlice and worms nesting there.
When you went, nothing happened. Everything did.

Release

I had to refrain from shaking you
restrain all feeling for your lying
in the mortuary, from crying out
as a spasm moved your mouth.

Midday, the doctor declared death
had released us from our watch:
had released you from such pain:
our watch is over, our pain remains

Locomotive Acts

will you walk before me
like the man with the flag
not surrendering but warning

Where?

If, as you say, there is no God,
nothing beyond this given rim
of earth once the dark funnels
flesh into itself, all is effluence,
a runnel, best left to nurture
future essence, nothing beyond
the incinerator: when I follow
where the fuck do I look for you?

After Her

Main St. is empty. Even the tardiest drunkard has caved into bed
his arm crooking the hardest hustler — who lacks a heart of gold,
diamonds etch deeper. They weave — don't all drunsters? —

their dreams together through this motherboard of night
prismatic with sick, chips, Rizlas leaking brown, a denuded
döner dressed in spit. Rats rifle it, pigeons shift as buildings

cool in the fade of a last star before the first stave of light scars
St. Bernard's hospital, warms newspapers stacked outside:
newspapers do not carry the tragedy — only the obituary.

Party

The noise raised the rafters but with 26 places laid -
Spanglish being the *lingua franca* and a white Rioja
vying for attention, defying a mere Sauvignon Blanc
to grace this table of deep-bodied pompano, scales
such a silver spangle we saw the rainbow trout look
to its colours, swore the whitebait winked at a crab,
so fresh it leapt onto the plate of its own accord, so
eager was he for the feast to begin and feast we did
each one surpassing his neighbour in wine and wild
tales, little wonder the rafters rocked to our laughter,
surely heaven heard and joined the toast as 25 rose,
Faustino Gran Reserva — what else could it be? —
red, gleaming (not only the wine) glasses held so high
even the angels cried *Salute* — we turned to our host:
      the chair empty. The plate turned down.

Returning

Despatched on the tarmac tourists negotiate
the carousel, sweep through cursory customs
head for Harrods, Fortnum's, Christmas sales,
quaver traditional carols around traditional tree,
unaware a Piccadilly line stop allows exodus
to suburbs where dark strokes a house hidden
in a cul-de-sac and the door hangs a wreath.

Encounter

Not here. Not in this place. But there.
Where a robin splayed his broken wing
and the shadow of the sparrow hawk
silenced small birds: the garden dark

with longing. Fig-purses spilled seeds
on dry earth, deciduous chokecherry
sought water. An intrigue of spite-sharp
nettle and leaf bled into uncut grass:

clawed at the gated door – red. Inside,
bolts rusted from disuse. Yet, even now,
a light flickers occasionally, a loose wire
seeking connection but the spy-hole stays
only one way: the one window ink-black.
Obsidian. There. It happened there.

Stable

How the heart closes
                         as the train slows
past Jim's tin roof of blue and yellow
panels taken from the breakers yard,
or day-trip trophies scavenged under
seagulls' eyes, hauled into his Morris,
tyres dragging over sand, suspension
sagging under this debris, leather seat
now definitely distressed, to be welded
one by one into a shelter: one last act
for the child whose snorting horse held
him high, who galloped to Samarkand
along the deep lake, past the big house,
small feet kicking its wooden flank, nails
studding poll to fetlock. *Faster! Faster!*

Declension

The house patient. Waiting. Gathering dark
in opaque windows that face both ways,
claw onto coarse grass where a woman
also waits, complicit, in this slow decline.

Look how the light falls, on the lake, he had cried,
rushing toward, unafraid, unaware of the strand's
                                              sudden shelving.

A psalm of leaves in wind is denied, only the anthem
to the day will be tolerated. She turns to where the sun
declines to leave shadows, to where windows on a far
shore glint at that water's edge: remain untouched.

Closure

Inside the dark eats the silence.
Inside he is diminished by her
touch to his hair, almost a tweak
– teasing; a butterfly kiss to side
of mouth – teasing: but at the light
spinal stroke running from his nape,

causing a frisson on his inner thigh,
he knows to be safe he needs control.
His heart stops on that moment, shifts
a little as trees shift when disturbed
or when a wind plays in the branches
that lift to the moon, scarring her face.

Negation

He wanted to leave
        a memorial
            but

He did not leave a body
                of work
He did not leave a clue
                to identity
He did not leave grieving
                relatives
(or none were found)

He left one trainer
            welt broken
he left behind inclement
              weather
He left behind a chalked
              outline
    removed by rain

Precipitation

You have to tread carefully in this place.
Keep your eyes lowered, your shoulders bowed
to guard against one false step which may lead
to your downfall.
                      Cars will cruise slowly past.
Behind their darkened glass you may catch
a glimpse of a whitened face. Look away.

Do not call out. You will be safe if you are not
a distraction. Their attention must remain fixed.
Any lack leads to a predictable consequence.
They will stop.
                  It may not be to your benefit.
Whether or not it is the usual signal designating
a road block, their primary target will remain.

They are wedded to the task in hand. Do not ask.
Simply proceed keeping to the left, or right, or indeed,
the centre. Move as if your life depended on it. It may do.
It is not only due to the ice.

Glass

The pane is the length of ceiling to floor
the door fixed to open slant a bare 9"

leaving it level with church spires naked
to the sky, no balcony in between

to intervene if a slim-hipped woman wishes to slip
through in a lather of grief at her loss

she is unable to contain: prefers to share
with passers by 14 floors below.

Guest

Behind the crinkle-crankle wall ropes
of rain and light litter the path. A crunch
of bones, the ring of fine glass unzipping
laughter, rankles the man who stands

at the edge. He has seen other bones,
another glass held to the light and so
he waits, knowing his presence awakens
other desires, the way the quiet of flesh

flinches to touch yet seeks its source,
the way a moment, untransformed,
pierces, demands immediacy, dulled
red of wine. He unfolds arms like wings.

Pliny: The Weight of Happiness

From the weight of them he could not say
whether the months had proved fortuitous
but selection and placement favoured true
assessment of the year's fortune, the way

another may make a small mark in a diary
denoting the sight of one whose happiness
he treasures or how Mr. Micawber's felicity
lay in addition or subtraction of a sixpence.

Today, dogs lie in the road to snap the bones
of hesitants as direction & diversions multiply,
while a dining penitent requests guidance on
which wine or bread to choose from the host
on offer: only wishing to avoid funeral meats.

Pliny noted that some customs put a black/white stone
in an urn to mark bad/good days, counted up at end of life.

Beach Huts

Uniform, they parade their stripes with all
bombast beyond the pier where light, cut
by a slash of rain, falls in uncertain folds,
the way a room mists at unexpected news,
the unexpected death: unforetold.

Hospice

for Marie

Grinning, Mick said he'd caught our salmon wading deep,
flicking the line hour after tireless hour, changing the fly
to see if a different treat tempted until finally, ceding victory
to the unseen fish, he threw himself belly-flat on the bank
to drop a lazy hand into the water, wrist through arm,
tickling the stones, when he felt a nip of finger and swiftly
seized the slipperiness, grasping what lay beneath, to bear it
triumphant, parade it through the streets with the village
gasping at the size, wondering how he could shoulder
such a weight and was it not a salmon but a seal in disguise,
a *silkie*, ran through the crowd, the pub turned out, the fiddler
stirring a tune in witness to Mick the victor.
                                                            You served thick slabs
cooked to a succulence we had never tasted, the skin crisp,
the fennel seeping into the flesh, the flesh flaking on our tongues,
saliva easing every mouthful, the fork clattering, eager to pinion
the next portion from your fine china plate where white asparagus,
tips tightly furled, paid court. The *Mâconnais* slipped past our lips,
Sancerre, saved from Easter feasting, teased, was preferred
to the more perfumed *Pouilly-Fumé* but all rapidly disappeared
with the last fleck of fish and the *craic* congratulating Mick
on the catch river-lifted today. Worth the early rising.
                                                                            Yes, you said.
Best be first in Gallagher's queue before another woman seizes
the brightest-eyed.
                You always were. And you did, said Mick. Grinning.

                * * * *

Take this with you and when it's my turn, drop down
this rope-word ladder to haul me up. I'll bring the wine.

Beggared

For if this is my sole inheritance –
to sift amongst pebbles on, say, Kerala

amongst people whose language I know not
but may yet learn, who will weave split willow,

tie with bark, cover in black tar and the black
hide from a prized bullock, the meat eaten,

shared with friends who help launch
the coracle in a shallow river, its oval shape

gliding between fish who gently nibble
alongside before sliding into the net

their glint of scales a lightstruck skitter
reflecting a sun that always shines –

then I would rather return to the bitter winter
scratch and bite inherent in her wild words.

Epilogue

To Whom It May Concern

Correspondence is the extradition of thought-word to a known/unknown
destination rendering the possibility for associative factors to be instigated
e.g. wood   board   water   waterboard   dead   deadwood   dead in wood
dead would assist elasticity retaining assertive migration of phonemes
to projective usage in performative territory, an integral process necessitating
structural rationale, the machinations of authorial intervention, applying kinetic
force, polemic discursive, self-referential avoidance, possibly cryptic parataxis.
                                  I shall never write to you again.

from *An Unfinished Sufficiency* (Salmon Poetry 2015)

RUTH O'CALLAGHAN, a Hawthornden Fellow, international competition adjudicator, interviewer, reviewer, editor, workshop leader and mentor, hosts two poetry venues in London, has compered and read at poetry festivals in the U.K. and abroad and has read extensively in Asia, Europe and the USA, and has collaborated with other disciplines and nationalities including Mongolian women poets (sponsored by Arts Council) which produced a book and CD. *Unportioned* is her tenth collection of poetry.

She has been awarded residencies in different European countries and at the XXX World Congress of Poets in Taiwan was awarded a gold medal. She has ten full collections and her book of interviews with internationally eminent women poets has been said to be "a very important contribution to world literary history." (Professor Clare Brant, University of London.)

Her two poetry venues, whose ethos is to promote poetry's social dimension, enables both famous and unknown to read together with proceeds contributing monies necessary to support two Cold Weather Shelters for the Homeless – the latter are also encouraged to participate. She endeavours to bring fresh audiences to poetry – especially those who are disadvantaged in some way. She has read to audiences of nearly a thousand in America where she was the only poet and the following day read on a buffalo farm where the buffalo outnumbered the audience. (One has to be flexible to be a poet.)

She is also the poet for Strandlines, a community, multi-disciplinary project administered by the auspices of Kings College, University of London.